Mr. and Mrs. Opposite

by Sylvia Root Tester
illustrated by Diana Magnuson

ELGIN, ILLINOIS 60120

Library of Congress Cataloging in Publication Data

Tester, Sylvia Root, 1939-
  Mr. and Mrs. Opposite.

  (Concept books)
  SUMMARY: A rhyming discussion of Mr. and Mrs. Opposite and their opposite personalities.
  1. English language—Synonyms and antonyms—Juvenile literature. [1. English language—Synonyms and antonyms]   I. Magnuson, Diana.   II. Title.
PE1591.T4   428'.1   76-45378
ISBN 0-913778-68-0

© 1977, The Child's World,. Inc.
All rights reserved. Printed in U.S.A.

Distributed by Childrens Press, 1224 West Van Buren Street, Chicago, Illinois 60607.

Mr. and Mrs. Opposite

There once lived a couple.
He was fat; she was thin.
He was short;
she was tall.
He liked to be out;
she liked to be in.

Her cat was old.

He liked hot foods;
she liked cold.

When she was good,
he was very, very bad;

which made him happy,
and made her mad!

When she was up,
 he was down.

He wore a smile;
she, a frown.

When she was dry,
he was wet.

Was she gleeful?
Was he mad?
You bet!

She ran fast;
he ran slow.

She hid high;
he searched low.

When he got on the ladder, she got off.

He landed on the hard ground; she found something soft.

She did whisper;
he did shout.
She did comfort;
he did pout.

She hurried up
and baked a cake.
She did give;
he did take.

Here's the happy ending; how can it miss?
Mr. and Mrs. Opposite
are sharing a kiss.

WITHDRAWN

NILES COMMUNITY LIBRARY